MICHAEL R. HOWARD

UNDER THE HELIX KELPIES

POEMS

Under the Helix Kelpies
Copyright © 2025 Michael R. Howard
ISBN: 978-1-970153-54-5
First Edition
Library of Congress Control Number: 2025901010
Printed in the United States
Distributed through Ingram Book Company

No part of this publication may be reproduced or transmitted in any form or by any means, graphic, electronic, photocopy, recording, or by any information storage retrieval system—except for excerpts used for published review—without the written permission of the author.

La Maison Publishing
Vero Beach, Florida
The Hibiscus City
lamaisonpublishing@gmail.com

"WHEN I'M GOOD, I'M VERY GOOD.
BUT WHEN I'M BAD, I'M BETTER."

                                        MAE WEST

For Mom and Dad

Introduction

The cover is a beautiful depiction of Scotland's iconic Helix Kelpies, the world's largest equine sculptures, created by artist Andy Scott. He has captivated the imagination as they "pay homage to the horses that once powered Scotland's industrial might." Although I was nearly killed on a horse at a young age, I remain loyal to and love all things related to horses.

Several poems in this collection have footnotes at the end of the poem. Hopefully, you will find this helpful.

Why the quote? Why not? I love quotes. There are no poems shorter, more concise, and more powerful than simple quotes. And how can you not love one by Mae West? There's a lot said in those twelve words.

Table of Contents

Under the Helix Kelpies 1

Rocks of Eriska 3

Greyfriars Bobby 5

Brown Dogs in a Green Field 7

Feral Kid 9

My Crested Caracara 11

Our Oasis – The Desert Inn 14

Florida Man vs The Gator 17

Hesperides Honey 20

With the Help of Hurricanes 22

My Own Rapa Nui 24

To Cut Down a Tree 26

Friday Night at D'Fly 28

His Trumpet Lesson 31

Waiting On the Blue Light 33

I Shall Remember 35

Our Siren Song 37

Promise on the Wall 39

Hungry, Patient Bags 40

Night Ship Attack	42
Tinian Twins	47
The Matriarch of the Dock	49
Island's Girl	51
Pier Chimp	53
Mill Village Boy	55
Caged	57
Baker's Bruises	59
The Saga of the Black Walnut Dilemma	61
After the Hunt	67
Partisan Patrol	68
Under the Osage	70
Acknowledgments	73

Under the Helix Kelpies
After Andy Scott's "The Helix"

The Helix spirals down from Langlees,
By River Caron and the Forth and Clyde Canal.
Here, two Kelpies stand guard each night
And by day, cast their silvery light.

> These Kelpies are benevolent shape-shifters,
> Water spirits who now have a home.
> They are a paean to all equines of yore
> Who once hauled coaches, hearses, and more.

The Clydesdale Carnera once strode these banks,
An equine who stood twenty hands high.
For years, he hauled whiskey and beer,
Now, the Kelpies embody him here.

> But he slipped on the cobbles of Cow Wynd.
> He fell there, and that did him in.
> Some said he took with him an era,
> But Scott's Kelpies will not let it end.

Those equines of yore transformed Falkirk,
And the Kelpies remind us of that past.
And what Scott so uniquely created,
Will allow that history to last.

Now the Falkirk wheel keeps turning,
And the locks still swell and drain,
And the heavy-weight champion of Falkirk,
Can forever smile from his grave.

This poem was a finalist in the 2024 Florida Writers Association's annual Royal Palm Literary Awards.

It was inspired by the actual "The Helix" – one of Scotland's most iconic landmarks, one of so many unique and beautiful places in my favorite foreign country.

Rocks of Eriska

I cross the old bridge to Eriska in Argyll,
Over tidal flats where the crannog hides.
Her shore rocks rest in the cradle of Loch Creran
And Stephenson's Light beckons across the bay,
Weakens the night's lonely mist and fog,
Then wakens the shore at break of day.

Here, Rae's otter rests in eternal bronze
Atop a rock, weaving smiles of schist and slate.
His white-stone horse bathes in the clearest air,
Surrounded often by its true equine kind.

Rae's stoic-stone Highland Cow
Guards the links with its timeless place and
Keeps watch on the distant Mountains of Mull
As the water-nymph island sleeps beneath its weight.

I caress the bronze otter and stone Highland Cow,
Gently stroke the white withers of his horse and
Daydream on a layered rock of Eriska's shore.

What wee wean spirit folded their colored clay
To make these swirling rocks of Eriska?
And why dress them in Loch Linnhe's yellow moss?

Then, from the cairn on Eriska's highest hill,
I see a wean playing among the shore rocks below.
That wean is me, and I have the clay in my hands.

This poem attempts to honor the natural beauty and mystic splendor of the Island of Eriska in Scotland. I visited there in 2023 and someday hope to return.

Greyfriars Bobby

In Greyfriars Kirk on Candlemaker Row,
They laid to rest John Gray.
His Bobby lay down beside him there,
And never went away.

Auld Jock, (John Gray), lay down there first,
Consumption had made him pay.
A Nightwatchman he was, his job well done,
But cold Edinburgh had her way.

Nightwatchmen had their watchdogs.
A Skye Terrier stuck with Gray.
Their rounds they made together each night,
Thru cold streets of snow and rain.

They fed Bobby tea and biscuits,
When once he lay down with Gray.
And promised him warmth from every hearth,
But wee Bobby did not stray.

Fourteen years he stood his watch
On the grave of ole John Gray.
The Kirkyard was his only home and
By his Master he always stayed.

All marveled at the wee dog's will.
All marvel at him still.
And when he died, all shed a tear,
For the grand ole Bobby dear.

Bobby touched the heart of every Clan,
Long before his final breath.
But when he died, he touched the heart,
The kind heart of a Baroness.

She shed many a tear for Bobby dear,
And from granite had him cast.
He'd stay with Gray in Greyfriars Kirk,
His watch in stone would last.

Now all tears fall eternal,
From the fountain of Bobby dear.
And ole John Gray rests forever,
With Greyfriars Bobby near.

A tribute to Greyfriars Bobby, the Scottish Skye Terrier, who guarded the grave of his master, John Gray, for 14 years. John Gray was buried in Greyfriars Kirkyard (Greyfriars Church Cemetery) in 1858 in Edinburgh, Scotland. Bobby was buried beside him in 1872.

Brown Dogs in a Green Field

A rising sun throws my long shadow
Down the dirt road.
It runs away westward
But will not get far and will
Come back to me soon enough.
A night's rain cleared the fall air and gives
A clean crispness to the tapestry
Of greens and browns,
Soon to give way to more vibrant colors.
The grass in the field is low, but thick, and
Will lay down and rest with the first frost.

I have one leg propped on the fence and
I am shielded from the cool morning breeze
By the thick skirt of an old cedar.
It drips dew as if just showered and
Its fragrance makes me long
For an afternoon gin, still a hard day away.
Hot coffee warms my hand.
The dogs led me out, raced ahead,
Eager for new morning smells in the field,
Left from whatever moved there in the night.

Damp grass holds scent best, and
The rising sun conjures up a fine mist
That swirls ghost-like around them.
Their breath is hard-earned and
Earnest tails signal smiles buried deep in the grass.
They are young, strong, and handsome
Brown retrievers who work the field.
An instinctive tandem, they share a scent,
Dig out clues, process them like a crime scene.
They are their own forensic team, and

With noses distilled through decades,
They dissect the DNA of forest and field.
This is where these brown dogs belong,
Long to be, and where their dreams take them
When they twitch and moan in the night.
All too soon winter will set in and dull these fields.
But this wide-faced pasture canvas,
Brush-stroked now by this brown tandem,
I will store in a place to recall with a smile,
Once my own frost and winter set in.

This poem was a finalist in the Florida Writers Association's 2024 Royal Palm Literary Awards.

Feral Kid

Where's your momma boy

> Somewhere out I spose
> But it don't matter
> You don't matter neither mister
> I'll throw a rock thru that window if I wanna
> I'll throw a rock at you
> You cain't catch me

You just a feral kid
I know you boy
I know your momma
You'll catch hell
When you git home

> I ain't going home
> Ain't got no home
> Ain't got no momma
> This is my home
> Now come on dog
> Leave that cat alone
> Lay down under this apple tree
> I'll be down in a minute.
>
> Then we'll go shoot an arrow straight up
> Steal some cigarettes
> Beat up that fat kid
> Throw rocks at that farmer's cow

Where's your poppa boy

> Gone, you otta know that
> You don't know nothin' mister

I know you ain't a good kid
All them other boys said they did it
But not you, but I know you was there
A good kid woulda said he was there
You just a feral kid

> You don't know nothin' mister
> I'm gonna go smoke a cigarette
> Ain't nothing you can do 'bout it

I outta beat the tar outta you boy

> Well, you ain't gonna
> Come on dog
>
> Let's go steal some liquor
> Let's go look in Sarah's bedroom window
> Let's go scare old lady Johnson
> Let's go set that field on fire

Why, you just a feral kid

> You don't know nothin' mister

My Crested Caracara

He don't look like he belongs 'round here,
Like he should be listed with those
Damn pythons down in the 'Glades,
Or that loathsome Brazilian Pepper tree
That'll grow right thru your pool screen.

Gotta cocky, arrogant look,
If you catch a rare glimpse of him,
Out off Highway 60, on top of some old fence post,
Statue-like, looking for some meal to chase down,
Or a free one on the road that ain't going nowhere.

They say he's fairly common
South of the border.
But he ain't common 'round here. And
He ain't got but a small place to hunt now,
Mostly just Osceola County.

I'm always glad to see him
When I pass by, and I like to think,
He's glad to see me, too,
And takes time for me on that fence post,
Where I always know to look for him.

He ain't like the Ospreys on the coast
And around the lakes where
I counted twenty of 'em on that causeway once.
He ain't like red-tail hawks that cycle thru and
Amp up squirrel and rabbit anxiety, and

Eagles are sorta rare, but familiar.
We know where all their nests are.
And Swallow-Tails pass thru like snowbirds
Just to soften up our skies.
No, he's Falcon-like, says a book.

But you won't see him soaring,
Too dignified for that.
Gonna stand on that fence post and pose,
Boldly wear his black beret, white neck scarf,
And spotted shoulder shawl.
Part matador and Frenchman.
Eccentric, iconic, eclectic, I'd say.
I guess by definition, he's a Raptor, a Bird of Prey.
But not an aerial hunter. Well,
Ain't you something, Mr. Threatened Caracara!

Well, I cain't soar with your cousins,
And neither can you.
But I can run and hunt on the ground with you.
So, take me with you thru those
Thick cabbage palms and saw palmetto,

Past the high cypress and scrub oak,
Thru the wet prairies and pastures.
I'll paint my face bright orange,
My nose, striking silver, like you.
Most dignified hunters we'll be, indeed.

Although the Crested Caracara is common throughout Central and South America, they are becoming threatened in their relict population of Central Florida. They are beautiful birds of prey with unique coloration and hunting habits. It's always a special thrill to see one perched on a fence post along Highway 60 somewhere in Osceola County.

Our Oasis – The Desert Inn

It was our oasis once, that ole Desert Inn.
But ain't much there now in Yeehaw Junction.
The girls there were purtty, smelled good,
And the beer was cold, most of the time.
The pine tar and cowshit washed off there
Better'n any other place in Osceola County.

I could go clear 'cross state on Highway 60,
Or take Kenansville Road, north or south.
But it was dang hard not to stop for a spell
At old Jackass Crossing, at The Desert Inn.

It wasn't no Las Vegas Desert Inn.
But I prob'ly lost more money in Yeehaw.
I thought I'd marry one of them pertty ladies once.
But she up and left 'for I could round up
All them cattle out on that prairie.

And when you go cuttin' them pines,
You start thinking hard 'bout that cold beer,
And them sweet smellin' girls back
At our oasis, The Desert Inn.

They put up a nice sign once, out front.
Said it was a *his-toe-rick* place.
Said we cowboys and pine cutters
Use to come here for supplies. Yea, we did.
But we come up here for more'n that. Yeehaw!

A big ole truck plowed into our oasis once.
Said it was carrying a load'a orange juice.
Well, I 'spose that was the next best thing to carry
'Sides our cattle and lumber.

Maybe that driver had a little too much vodka
With all that orange juice he was carrying, yeehaw.
Maybe he was just in a hurry to get back
To the oasis, …back to The Desert Inn.
I always got good gator tail and turtle burger there,
And their swamp cabbage was always hot.

Sometimes I rode in with Jefferson or Billie Blue Coat,
But I couldn't eat with 'em. They had a separate place.
I never understood that, 'cause
We worked them same cows and
Cut them same pines together.
Them cows didn't care what color we was.

I was glad I got back there again 'fo that truck driver.
It was quiet for a while inside.
And we had a few warm beers.
And then it got dark, and the music come up.
And then I thought I saw
That ole lady I wanted to marry.
Had her arm around some ole cowboy,
And they was laughing,
And swaying their way back
To one of them ole cabins.

Later on, I thought I heard a gunshot or two.
And a fight broke out. The po-lice came,
But they never took nobody away.
And they was always careful
Not to check them rooms.
And the register, well,
Sure had a lot of Smiths and Jones sign in
At our oasis - The Desert Inn.

Located at Yeehaw Junction, Florida, The Desert Inn was added to the U.S. National Register of Historic Places in 1994. In 2019, a tractor-trailer crashed into the Desert Inn and destroyed it. As of October 2024, it remains a pile of rubble, and it is highly unlikely that it can ever be restored.

Florida Man vs The Gator

I travelled a long way to find Florida Man.
But it was worth it.
"Florida Man – He has things under control."
I wanna be Florida Man,
Swim fearless in "The River of Crawling Death."
Wrap my arm tight around
That lovely maiden in distress,
Keep her shirt from flying fully open.

Well, maybe not that tight.

And who says, "Engineers make better lovers?"
Maybe she said that…Maybe she knows.
Florida Man better be an engineer.

I hung Florida Man with all my other Florida scenes.
But he gets the best reaction.
Everybody loves Florida Man.

But then Hugh caught my eye.
Hugh just sat there like a stoic,
Smoked his pipe with a calm grin,
Like he just made love to one of his playmates.
Yea, he smoked after sex.
And he never had to visit the Space Coast.
He was never a "Love-starved vacationist."
Everybody envies Hugh,
Even Florida Man.

Later I went to the big show.
But neither Hugh or Florida Man were there
And I was greatly disappointed.
Then, I was soon bitten by the gator.
He'd been there all along, just hiding in plain sight.
Gators are like that: sneaky, stealthy, patient.
Yea, neither Hugh or Florida Man
Stand a chance with this gator,
Especially in that "River of Crawling Death."
I'll just put Florida Man back on my wall
Where everyone can marvel at him.

But the gator, how can I take him home?
He's bold. He commands the room.
And he can drag you into deep water,
Rip you to shreds and eat you.

I like that. I want this gator.
But I can't take a gator home.
He'd just hide there like gators do,
Patient, stealthy, waiting to bite.

He needs to be seen.
And I don't want to tread lightly
Around the house to
Avoid being ripped to shreds and eaten.

I'll just stick with Florida Man.
He and I can swim in that
"River of Crawling Death" any time we want.
We'll make our own — Wild Times.

Yeah, this one needs a little explanation. This is an ekphrastic poem inspired by an old replica magazine cover I found at the gallery of artist Derek Gores, whose studio is located in Eau Gallie, Florida. In the poem, I reference two other works of art by Derek: "Wild Times" and the "Hugh Hefner" Playboy cover. Our writing group collaborated with Derek for an ekphrastic event during his exhibition at Gallery 14, Vero Beach, Florida, in March 2024. Had I been able to include the "Florida Man" cover with this poem, it would make perfect sense.

Of note - Derek created the cover of Playboy Magazine's special tribute edition to Hugh Hefner shortly after Hugh's death in 2017. Derek's "brand of pop surrealism is immortalized in vintage colors on the cover of Playboy's 120-page special tribute edition to Hefner's legacy." Check out Derek's incredible and unique work on his website at "DerekGores.com."

Hesperides Honey

There is little here in Hesperides, Florida.
Green carpets of citrus are gone:
Left in a hurry, like desperate renters
Who leave in the night, deep in debt.

What took the citrus, also took that sweet
Scent of grapefruit which once lingered
Heavy here to perfume Hesperides air,
Nymph-like touched on neck and wrists.

Perhaps those Golden Apples grew here once,
Thick, in a lovely garden guarded by dragons.
I look for those dragons when I pass through,
But feel only their blistering breath.

Would those Golden Apples grant my immortality?
The name Hesperides suggests they should be here.
Here, where evenings are sweetened, too,
By the golden light of their guarded sunsets.

But it's just a silly tease,
Except for the honey of Hesperides,
Which you can get with ease.
Just stop at the sign before you leave.

Hesperides, Florida – blink, and you'll miss it. What a great name for a town and another gem on Highway 60. Though the citrus is gone, the honey is still there. Blink and you'll miss it, too. I seldom pass it by.

With the Help of Hurricanes

I stumbled out of Pat O'Brien's
After too many Hurricanes.
As I left their Flaming Fountain behind,
I wondered why I was asked to leave.
I had only tried to kiss one
Of the dueling piano players.

Outside, on hot, crowded St. Peters,
She appeared like a tropical island
To a man adrift at sea.
Our eyes locked, and I saw only
Her singular beauty, all else a blur.
I went to her straightaway,

Threw my arms around her, kissed her,
And proclaimed she was with me now,
Like a pirate boldly claiming stolen treasure.
"Be Bold and Great Forces Will Ally With You"
But the phrase does not include
"With the Help of Hurricanes."

We snaked our way thru the Mardi Gras crowd,
Found refuge on the hood of a car,
Kissed passionately until an annoying tap, tap, tap
Of something heavy on my shoulder
Made me turn into
Strong words suggesting
I not do this on the hood of his squad car.

So, my beauty and I snaked our way
Down Bourbon Street,
My hurricane swagger intact.

But, as my hurricane ferocity waned,
I knew I could not hold this
Jewish princess with such feline-like freedom.

Once though,
with the help of hurricanes,
I stood boldly in the eye.

Mardi Gras 1977 at the iconic Pat O'Brien's of New Orleans and its signature drink "The Hurricane."
I remember enough to write this.

My Own Rapa Nui

The new hay bales stand patient,
Randomly strewn across the rolling pasture,
Unflinching under a straight-up sun,
Hard rains and cold nights.
A pole's dull light bends their shadows
Like a *van Gogh* glow, long and lean,
Down toward the creek.

My Moai, here on my own Rapa Nui.

They are fall sentinels, ignoring
Inquisitive crows who strut at their feet like tourists
Who look up in awe, then move on.
The morning coaxes weak steam from their backs,
Like exhaled breath or the mist
Which lifts from the hides of hot cattle
After a passing summer squall.

My Moai, here on my own Rapa Nui.

My Moai stare, keep watch, intimidate
With singular, unblinking eyes.
They are grass, eaten and digested by merciless
Creature-like machines which deposit them like horse droppings.
Transformed into giant, neat rolls,
They clutch the grass, string-tied and wrapped,
Ready to feed those who feed us.

My Moai, on my own Rapa Nui.

I want my Moai to stay.
But they have work to do and must go.
They leave promise that the grass
Will grow tall again and
More will come later to once again become

My Moai on my own Rapa Nui.

Rapa Nui is the native name for Easter Island. Moai are the carved monumental human figures found on Easter Island.

To Cut Down a Tree

I once cut down a tall, yellow poplar
With a small, red-handled hatchet.
It towered high above all others and to cut it down
Seemed the thing to do, like a rite of passage.

I did not plant its seed, water it, nurture it.
I took no part in its growth.
I never pruned it, or cleared around
To give it light, advantage, and help to fight through
Choking vines and creepers
And all things that compete.

Yet, it fought its own way up
Through thick brush and dark foliage,
Through dry summer heat and flood.
It grew tall, straight, and high above the rest.

My endeavor was hard and earnest. But,
I took its life with careless thought and
As it crashed through all those it had eclipsed,
I felt my folly and knew I could not forget this.

I clawed my way through
Its thick mass of angry limbs and leaves,
Their final act to prevent my way to its heart,
As if to protect the last breath of the dying monarch.

Then I knew I could not process such a glorious thing,
Not with a small, red-handled hatchet.

I hear it crash and rip even now,
As if it screamed on the way down,
Holding on, clinging, resisting that inevitable end,
To lie helpless and slowly rot on the forest floor,
Like a dethroned, banished King.

I stared helpless, too, at this innocent, virtuous tree
As it sparkled in the hot sun.
The whiteish underside of its leaves quivered
As the leading wind of a summer storm approached.

If only the swarm of developers had a similar ounce of regret or alternatives to leveling our forests and woodlands.

Friday Night at D'Fly

It's Friday night at The DragonFly,
Or just "D'Fly" late at night
When the empty bottles and glasses stack up.
Musicians meet here and
Appraise the band in whispers;
Their language as foreign to me as French.
But their words and the music sooth my starved ears.
So, I soak up each riff and song and
Try in vain to reconcile their earnest critiques,
While the band hammers on to my heart's rhythm.
Their songs are hypnotic and I focus on
Some lovely ladies close by,
Whose bodies say sultry things I fully understand
As they sweat and sway in the dim light.

It gets dark early. So, I sit longer at the bar
And cold Red Oaks fuel my dying inhibition.
I look far past the band through blurred vision,
Out through smoke-aged windows,
Which hold in the drummer, but not his thunder.
With his back to the glass, he hammers on.
I wanna hammer, too,
And another empty glass makes it clear,
Tomorrow, that's the one thing I'll do.

I look further, to the old Court House,
Far across a smoke-hazed sidewalk
And an American Graffiti Street to

Where Earl Scruggs holds court,
With just his three-fingered banjo.
I pause briefly on his courthouse lawn
Where thick grass invites a rest
Under ancient, long-shadowed oaks.
And even there, you feel D'Fly's vibes.

Then, my focus drifts back inside,
Slides past eager young men outside
Spilling beer on a thirsty sidewalk,
Forcing smiles and gestures on the girls
Whose skin-tight, spandex slaps,
(Or whatever they're called)
Makes me smile and whisper to my friend;
"I pray this fashion never ends."
Then, on every sculpted rear end,
We both focus and zero in.

The black house cat eases past,
Inspects me with an indifferent pass,
Ready to swipe a scratch across my hand
Should I try to be a friend.
Cigar racks and wine shelves are ignored
And the tip jar gets more attention than
Big Foot and James Dean who stand alone in back.
It's the sweating sets and active taps
Which capture this Friday night.

The owner prowls, knows us all,
He's the patron saint of D'Fly.
His curly, red-head mate makes her rounds, too.

I wager she's as fierce as that black cat.
Tonight, it's blues, tomorrow country,
Next week it's reggae or rock.
You cain't go wrong at the bar in back.
But give it a try. You at D'Fly.

The "DragonFly" is in downtown Shelby, N.C. I have a reserved seat there on Friday nights with my accomplished musician cousin.

His Trumpet Lesson

He blasts out his pain
From a body, stiff as a trumpet's brass tubes and
Filled with enough metal to build his own Bach.
Shape its valves from the rod down his spine,
Its bell, slides, and rings from parts in his hips.
Use the old parts, too, kept thru the years,
Worn out, replaced with new.
Reminders for all the sharp notes he needs.

His mute muffles the tone of his late-night moans
Like a fist in the mouth to bite and stifle
The sting of a mortal wound.
It tempers the volume and tone
For the well-tuned ear
But cannot dampen his grimace, his flinch.
The limp, the stiff agony,
Disappear like sweet notes of a favorite tune

As his music soothes and softens his torment
Like new metal in hips, neck, and spine should do.
But they are always off-key.
He inserts a new mouthpiece
To change the pitch, alter the melody,
And blasts out his pain, distilled,
Weakened, when shared with an audience
Overcome by the force and beauty of his lesson.

My first cousin, Christopher Cole, is an accomplished and gifted musician who is in the North Carolina Bandmasters Association Hall of Fame. He has endured incredible orthopedic challenges his entire life, and I lost track of the number of surgeries he's undergone. I meant for this poem to be a tribute to his skill as a musician, his constant optimistic approach to life, the physical challenges he has overcome throughout his life, and the success he has achieved in spite of these challenges. A lesser man would have given in long ago. I am so proud of him. This poem doesn't do him justice and I wish I were a better poet to honor him more appropriately. But it is filled with love and admiration. Maybe that helps a little.

Waiting On the Blue Light

Each morning, I wait on the blue light
Which tells me coffee is ready.
It's a simple light that turns from red to blue.
I like the wait. It's not long.
While I wait, I think about the low-blue flame
On my grandmother's old gas stove.
It kept her morning coffee boiling till noon and
Leached every ounce of flavor from grounds
Tortured in the dark innards of her ancient pot,
A distilling process not unlike good whisky.
She was familiar with that, too.

The moment I entered her house,
The aroma of boiling coffee hit me like a fist.
An instant headache ensued with
The air so thick I would hack my way
To her kitchen with an imaginary butcher knife,
Where she sat and read the morning paper,
Every word, as her pot exhaled hot steam and
Burped angry brown in its one glass eye,
As if to give me an all-knowing wink.

She was old and the stove, too far away.
So, she would ask me to "warm" her coffee,
Which really meant to pour her another cup
Of boiling black coffee, hot enough to scald her cat,
Which I often considered.

I did not drink coffee for a long time after that.
But somewhere along the way things changed.
Maybe the genes I inherited from her led me to it
And was in my DNA all along,
And those headaches were just my body's way
Of stripping the unneeded parts of my soul
To expose that true need for scalding hot caffeine.
Now, I often drink it all day, like she did.

***

But I can never find coffee as hot and strong as hers.
I've yet to find a coffee shop or machine
Which can distill and heat coffee
Like her one-eyed monster
And give me that aroma-induced headache.
And thankfully, I've not had to simulate
Hacking my way to its counter with a butcher knife.

So, I bought my own pot with one glass eye
And one small light
Which turns blue when the coffee is ready.
They laugh at my simple, new pot,
And heads shake as I sit and wait on that blue light.
And when they're gone,
I "warm" my own coffee and enjoy the headache.
It's always hot enough to scald our cat.
Which I often consider.

I Shall Remember

I shall remember
Mrs. Nell Carpenter bringing (the news)
As long as I have life to hold
In moments bright or blue.

I shall remember all we once did
To please and comfort each other
And how you were the pattern
For each golden memory.

When I go walking or stand,
I shall recall how sweet it was
To hold your gentle hand
And look into your eyes
And hear you whisper secrets
For my heart to memorize.

I shall remember how
We dreamed and waited
For each dawn
Until I touched a shadow and
I knew that you were gone.

Monnie Blanton

This was written by my maternal grandmother. It was written by pencil on a faded yellow sheet of old notebook paper. I found it just recently, folded up and hidden away among the immense amount of treasures my late mother collected and kept throughout her life. Along with it was the last letter my grandmother wrote to her husband, my grandfather, while he worked in the Norfolk or Portsmouth shipyard and just prior to his fatal car wreck on his way home. I can only presume the letter was found among his personal effects at the scene and returned to his family. This was in 1941.

What amazes me about this poem is that I never saw my grandmother write anything. She'd had no formal education at all, and I never knew or thought that she could write. She never talked about my grandfather and kept her grief personal and deep. She never remarried. I am so deeply touched and moved by this simple little poem. I miss her so much and cannot imagine her lifelong pain of being without her husband.

Our Siren Song

When first she sang, we ran to her.
She was our bitch and lived with us
In our Mad Max desert compound,
Within our wounded womb of concertina wire
Where missiles flashed across the night sky
Like lovely comets bringing death to earth.
But razor wire will not stop incoming missiles.
So, we dug a bunker deep in the desert sand.
And then, when they came, she sang. We ran.
But she sang too often, too loud, and badly,
And was very jealous of our sleep,
What little we found. And soon,
Her song faded into our bad dreams,
And we never ran to her again.

She was ancient, unique, her origin unknown.
And once she began to sing, no one dared claim her.
She just appeared and I envisioned her former life,
Strapped to the top of an old fire engine
As it sped through a crowded city to a five-alarm fire.
She clung there beside
The spotted, barking Dalmatian,
As a fireman earnestly cranked out her dreadful song.

Though she eventually sang to us in vain,
She was never dissuaded,
Always diligent and devoted.
And at the end, she disappeared

As mysteriously as she arrived.
I wanted to take her home where she could sit quietly,
Rest peacefully, a conversation piece and
I would make her sing on special occasions.
But sirens are not like that. They must sing,
To someone, somewhere, forever, I suppose.

I often wonder where she sings now,
And to whom?
And do they run to her for a while,
Until she steals their sleep,
And her song fades into their bad dreams.

During Desert Storm someone found an old hand-cranked siren. Yes, you literally had to wind it up to wake it up and get it going. Useless, really. But a unique and humorous thread to the fabric of war.

Promise on the Wall

The peach tree has brown rot disease.
It kills each peach at their prime:
Fat, ripe, and holding such promise.

Every day I count the fallen, which
Oddly makes me think back to Vietnam,
When the news served up the daily body count.

My cousin had himself ordained then,
To avoid the draft. He was not a minister,
Just a long-haired hippie, but he held such promise.

He's in lockdown now.
When I visit him, a nurse lets me in.
Later, he won't remember I was there.

Once, I searched the Vietnam Wall for his name.

I knew it was not there. I just wanted it to be,
There, among all the others
Who held such promise.

Hungry, Patient Bags

The body bags are black, thick, and rubbery.
Open and empty with heavy-duty zippers,
They yawn with a hungry, patient look.

Clean and new, they are unloaded at night,
An attempt to be discreet. But it's a half-hearted effort
To stack them neatly. Everyone is in a hurry to finish.

I reach out to touch one. But resist.
They are not what I expected.
They were not expected.

Are there names already inside?
Which of my boys will we tuck inside,
Like we gently tuck our children in at night?

Where will they gather after?
How will they get home?

I have seen old photos of our boys
Laid out in neat rows.
Their faces visible, sometimes recognizable.
They were free to be seen and mourned. Not in bags.

No, don't unload anymore.
We will lay our boys out to be seen, to be honored,
Where our tears can drop
And christen their blackened faces.

Get the hell outta here! Zip up your yawning bags.
You are not welcome here. You are not needed here!
We don't want you, you hungry, patient bags.

Night Ship Attack

It is vacant—black and cold.
Here, well below the dark water's surface
I find myself focused on an eerie glow,
As if from some hazy, distant galaxy.
It allows me to read a small compass
And other instruments,
When held close to my face.

They are on a swimmer board,
The size swimmers use in pools
To strengthening their kick.
But mine is deep under water
And we are not at swim practice.
I steer and swim us in the path the compass demands.
It is the only thing I believe in.

The slightest distraction will turn the needle.
There are no stars to guide us, no maps, no phones.
Satellites cannot reach us down here.
We watch our depth. There is a limit and
Death looms close below
Should we go deeper and linger.
A bitter mouthpiece is just one
Of many things that annoy.

I breathe back in my own exhaled breath
As it is recycled through the devise
I carry on my back.

I pray that my breath flows correctly
Through the chemical
I loaded earlier into the canister of my dive rig
And absorbs my exhaled carbon dioxide.
If all works correctly, there will be no bubbles

That reach the surface to explode and
Leave a visible trail
To announce our underwater approach.
The sound of breathing is hypnotic and mechanical.
I am tethered to another diver.
It is easy to separate and
Lose one another in the dark depths.
His hand gently grips the back of my upper arm.

It is comforting to know he is there.
Shared fear gives courage.
A frequent squeeze of my arm
Lets me know he is okay.
The water is cold, but a layer of rubber helps.
But any twist of my neck allows a trickle of water
To run down my spine
And reminds me just how close
To the ambient water we really are and that
We will not stay miserably comfortable for long.
The cold will soon seep in deep to our core.
Something streaks past, comet-like, in front of us and
Leaves a phosphorescence trail
That we swim through.
Whatever made it was large.

We ignore it and press on. We will talk about it later
And embellish the size of it, too.
I force myself to imagine
That it was just a startled fish.
But my mind dances with bigger
And more dangerous things
That swim here in the night.

I force myself to think of mundane things
To counter the creeping fear, the numbing cold.
I focus on the course, the depth,
The squeeze on my arm, the rhythmic breathing.
These are enough for now.
These are enough to push down the fear
While strong legs pump my fins
Like a hydraulic machine.

The fear will ramp up soon.
The ambient noise of shrimp and crabs
Clicking in the night depths
Are familiar, comforting sounds.
But they begin to fade as
The sounds of a living ship take shape.
It pumps, throbs, and turns things inside and out.
They are its living sounds:
Breathing, heart pumping, bowels emptying.

They are fearful sounds
For it fears no one and will eat anyone.

I fear the noise.

But fear is good, makes me concentrate.
I want to believe this. I try to believe this.
The noises grow louder and we know we are close.
The water feels alive.
It seems to vibrate in a strange way.
I hit solid steel. A wall of steel.
We stop kicking, ease deeper,
Feel our way along a hull that we cannot see.

There is slick slime on the hull and barnacles that cut.
It is near impossible to know
Which way to the bow or stern.
We could easily feel our way in the wrong direction.
It is a very large ship and
I imagine us under a football field,
Blindfolded, feeling our way along its grass roots,
Trying to find the goal line,
Not knowing our start point.

With luck, we find its keel, its aorta, its spine.
Our knees are on the bottom, in the mud.
Our heads bang against the hull above us.
We're forced to crouch, bend over.
It is awkward, uncomfortable work.
It is cave-like. I fight off the claustrophobic feeling
Creeping in around me like a cage.

The compass no longer works
Under such massive steel.
It is all done by feel.
Even the heavy silt we stir up does not matter.

We see it only because
We must pull our depth gauge close.
I somehow remember that the tide is coming in.
So, the ship will not settle further,
Will not settle on us,
Will not push us down into the mud.
Focus now, focus.

Ignore the fear. We have a job to do.
We trace the keel
To the massive shafts, screws, and rudders.
This is where we need to be,
Where we will kill or wound this massive beast.
Where it might kill or wound us.
This is its Achilles heel,
And ours.

This is a common tactic for Navy SEALs (aka, Combat Swimmers). But there's a lot left out here.

Tinian Twins

We see just yards ahead as vines and clawing things
Seek our blood thru sweat-soaked shirts.
A narrow path on old, dark-stained concrete tells us
We are on one of the twin runways.
Neither fully visible,
We weave our way thru thick tropical growth,
Pressed in and heavy with distilled, humid wetness.
Wild papaya grows thick and drops its rotting fruit,
Adding to the sickly-sweet, sweating air.
The twins live in a far-away place,
Unknown when born, forgotten now.
There was little here then, less now.
And a plaque, desperate for attention,
Explains their birth,
Largest, quickest project ever, ever still.
Things like this are possible,
When you need to kill.

They stretched their white-bright arms once,
Straight across this thin island and
Threw young men as far as Japan
Who ascended into the distant clouds
And took with them a new horror
Named victory, peace, the ignoble end.
It was but a moment's thriving endeavor.
Then death and destruction fell silent
And we gave them to the island's care.
Time and nature aged them.

Remote and unneeded,
They hide like a Pharoh's treasure
Waiting under the onslaught of
Jungle rot and counting years.

Once, they made a fine pair here.
Now, they rest together, but never really sleep.
One day, perhaps soon,
We will sweep clear the decades,
Add new life to the Tinian Twins.
For death and destruction, like old concrete,
Lasts forever.

Tinian and its twin runways are indeed making a comeback. They are being revitalized as a deterrence to China's growing threat and they may well be used again. It is a dreadful thought.

The Matriarch of the Dock

The marina is asleep now and still.
The Matriarch of the Dock passed away
Quietly in the night.
Summer's Strawberry Moon
Lifted her gently into its soft, silvery light
As it ambled across the dark sky and
Cast its white magic on the wide tidal flats below.
But she, The Matriarch of the Dock,
Will visit us here on the dock again,
When each full moon sweeps the marsh,
Swells the tide,
And fills the river's veins with her goodness.

Then, we'll hear the dock swing creak
In evening's quiet.
We'll think it pushed by the wind. But,
It will be the gentle touch of her unseen hand.
And the Julienton will flood full to pay respects,
And cover the grieving sandbar across the river,
Which cannot bear to see her empty cup and chair
That together, each morning, they would share.
The noisy grackle will hush with sadness,
The mullet will jump and
Softly splash their sympathies.
The herons, too, will halt their quiet hunt.
And all will pause in silence.

There will be far too many weeping eyes to count,
With tears sufficient to fill Sapelo sound,
Whose river will carry them far from the Bluff,
Far past the sad boats moored in silent prayer,
Their halyards tinkling her favorite tune,
Far enough to salt the shores of St. Catherines.

But the marina will wake with each full moon.
And The Matriarch of the Dock will
Turn the tide and uncover the bar,
Swing the young in the shade again.
The grackle will boast his presence.
The herons will resume their hunt.
The Julienton will flow out again, and strong,
And takes with it our grief, which we will freely give,
For only the tide can carry this.

A tribute to the model for all mothers, a grand lady who passed in 2024 at age 94. I loved her very much.

Island's Girl

He stood there on the shore like a stoic,
Arms folded, holding tight his grief.
He'd waited for her thru the long, hot day.
The shadows finally touched him,
As if to gently soothe his anguish,

The sun ignored him all day, too,
But began to settle and quit its hateful
Alliance with the morning's horror.
So, now, he waited.
Now, it was just a long vigil:
A valiant watch seaward
Into dark waters, an approaching tide,
And the eternal, indifferent surf.
He would wait till we found her.
She was now the island's girl.

Perhaps a dolphin would swim her in.
He'd heard they do that sometimes,
Save someone.
She'd come back, arm outstretched,
Hand clutched on its dorsal fin,
Giggling at the fun ride thru a gentle surf
On the back of a strong, wise creature.

Or maybe a beguiling mermaid
Would swim her in, smile up from the white foam,
Laugh, "It was all just for fun," she'd say.
And push the island's girl into the shallows
Where she could stand, walk to him,
Smile at him, speak to him again.
But no dolphin or mermaid would come now.
They would not bring him the island's girl.

He could not see her. But she was there.
We knew it. We would find her.
He would be grateful.

Then the boy beside me said,
"Here she is."
And we pulled her up
And carried her to the beach,
And to him.
The tepid waters washed away
From her ashen face.
He gently pushed away her dark hair
That gathered across her brow.
I wanted her to reach up, smile,
And brush away her own hair.
But she was now the island's girl.

A true depiction of a father's anguish knowing his young daughter had drowned. This occurred on Jekyll Island in the early 1970s. I was a Beach Lifeguard on duty far from the tragedy but was called upon to help recover her body.

Pier Chimp

The chimp held his cigarette in a mouth with no lips,
Precarious, like one of those free climbers
Who hangs from a high ledge with one hand.
Made me anxious, nervous.
I couldn't hold one like that.

He sat quietly in his tight cage at the head of the pier,
Chain-smoked cigarettes, given by
Passing tourists and fishermen.
There to attract the curious,
He did his job well.

I walked a long way down the beach
Just to see him.
Hot, barefoot, sunburned,
I first cooled off in the shade under the pier.
The chimp was not going anywhere.

Waves thundered into thick pilings,
Made the pier shudder.
I felt it when I walked on its hot,
Creosote-soaked boards.
The wind kept the pier boards dusted
With blowing beach sand.
Shade was sparse, splinters plenty.
All just part of the pier's misery.

I wanted to lock eyes with the chimp and look deep,

Search for common understanding.
Our DNA was nearly the same.
I wanted to convey my sympathy.
But our eyes seldom met.
When they did, I felt his contempt.

When his cigarette died
He searched each new
Hand and face for another.
Someone stuck a long-neck bottle
Through his chicken-wire door.
He grabbed the neck and drank.

I'd seen news stories
About pet chimps, who,
After years with their loving owner,
Suddenly went berserk and
Attacked them with vicious strength
And a preference for face and groin.
Unprovoked, one ripped its owner's face off.

But chimps were daring astronauts,
Gifted performers, and
Faithfully serve our medical profession.
Tarzan loved Cheetah,
Jane Goodall loves them all.
And our DNA is so nearly the same.

I saw this chimp at the head of a Myrtle Beach, S.C. pier many years ago.

Mill Village Boy

He stood in the dust
And looked at me,
That mill village boy
With the big head.

Always there, always distant,
Always in the same spot
Each morning, as if waiting just for me.
He stood away from the others,
Normal kids in the background,
Indifferent to their noise and movement.

He just stood there in the dust,
And looked at me.
That mill village boy
With a big head.

Sometimes he tilted his head,
A slight, quizzical move,
Like a dog at a strange noise.
But I was never sure.
Maybe he just needed to move
Such heavy weight.
Maybe he wasn't thinking at all.
But I wanted him to.
I wanted him to think deep thoughts.
Not just stand there in the dust

And look at me.
That mill village boy,
That kid with the big head.

I think I know him now,
Thru decades of memory
And the occasional nightmare.
That big-headed kid,
That mill village boy,
Standing in the dust,
Staring at me.

I thought I saw him once.
A man with a big head
Walked past me, looked at me,
Tilted his head, quizzical,
As if he remembered me.
But he kept on,
That man with a big head.

Caged

It came down quickly,
Surrounded the little bird,
Surprised and trapped it,
As if the little bird didn't mind,
Welcomed it, in some strange way.

After all, it is a brutal world out there,
And perhaps it wanted the shelter,
Food, water, and love. Ah yes, the love.
Everything in life is a tradeoff, I suppose.
But you give up a lot when caged.

As Emerson said,
"One must consider
What a rich realm one abdicates
When one becomes a conformist."

That wee one once sang sweetly
Outside our window, so free.
And friends often gathered to admire
Its strong wings, vibrant colors,
And unique song.

But once caged, it changed, as things do.
Now, its song, not as sweet,
Weakened wings, faded colors,
Reticent, no longer free to fly

High among soft clouds
Above ancient green fields and
Breathe the whiskey-soaked air
Of old pubs where it often nested.
And too far from the drummer

To feel the beat and heat of his heart.
It no longer drank from the fountain
In the cool evening where friends gathered.
A cage will not allow this.

I had a bird in a cage once,
A lovely Blue-Nape Parrot,
Sweet, gentle, liked to nibble on my ear,
A jungle parrot who talked.
But in time, its colors faded; its voice weakened.
It never flew again and slowly died.

Safe, fed, loved. Ah yes, loved.
Did it miss the lush, green, dangerous jungle,
And just maybe, confused freedom and love?

Baker's Bruises

She came home in tears, quiet, alone.
Her face bruised and swollen.
A quick retreat to their bedroom
Was an attempt to hide the truth.

Why am I not in there to help,
To comfort, to get answers?
But from outside the door,
I heard a name I knew well.

My rage heated like our stove-top.
I knew that name. I knew that bastard.
I will find him. I'll go.
I'll kill that SOB Baker.

I went. I took my fists. I never found him.
He fled to places I could not go.
He knew my rage, my intent.
You can't do things like that
To a boy's mother and walk away.

For years he stayed in my crosshairs.
But he died, far away, of some stupid illness.
My rage cooled to disappointment
But never to sympathy or forgiveness.

That was long ago and bruises heal.
But rage never completely cools and
Forgiveness just gets pushed down.
If I saw him today,
I'd kill that SOB Baker.

The Saga of the Black Walnut Dilemma

From where I sit and write
I clearly see the old Black Walnut tree.
It stands in the saddle of two pasture slopes,
Indifferent to the love-hate whims I exalt on it.
I care for it too often and far more than it deserves.
I trim its branches and cut vines that sneak and
Snake up its trunk each summer
In their relentless attempt to choke the life out of it.
I often think I should just leave them to their pursuit.
Or better, just cut the old tree down.
This would end all the many frustrations it spawns.
And there is always great value in its wood,
Highly favored by woodturners
For its hardness and beauty.
I could then build a small pond in that saddle,
Which, for decades, I have longed to do.
But I'm weak and can never see that threat through.

The tree also marks the spot, where long ago,
Now forgotten relatives built their home.
They probably planted this confounded tree.
Ground hogs, too, have occupied the site
And littered the ground with deep holes
Which hide in the thick grass and
Hold promises for sprained ankles and twisted knees.

This Black Walnut is the slowest tree
To bud and leaf each spring.
At times, I think it's dead. But it's just a tease.
It will eventually leaf out and take its place
Among all the others which
Hurried to leaf out and face the sun.
But this Black Walnut is like a sluggish old bear,
Slow to wake from hibernation,
Content to roll over and sleep a few more weeks.

Throughout the long, hot summer,
Its fruit grows slowly to the size of baseballs.
The inner nut meat lies convoluted
Deep within a hard shell,
Covered further by a thick outer husk.
This fruit drops in the fall and
Once on the ground, soon turns to a black mush.
If I didn't know better, I'd think they've rotted.
But no, I'm just getting started.
It's now time to pick 'em up.

I wear gloves that I can throw away.
They'll soon be stained black.
The husks stain everything black, even each other.
I gather them in an old croaker sack.
Then I take a baseball bat and beat the hell out of 'em.
No need to worry. This never cracks any nuts inside.
It just softens up the husks a little more.

Next, I pour them in the ruts
Of my well-used dirt road.
They lie there like discarded road kill.
I can rest awhile now and
Forget these dastardly Black Walnuts
And take joy in repeatedly
Running them over in the road.
This gives a lot of pleasure, but it's temporary.
They have plenty more frustration to give.

Several weeks later,
If I haven't deliberately forgotten them,
And the squirrels haven't decimated them,
I go pick up all that road kill,
And dump it into an old washtub.
I crank up the pressure washer
And blast the black walnuts
Hard enough to take paint off the Sistine Chapel.
This removes the remaining husks but,
It's a nasty business.
Bits of rotting black husk fly everywhere,
And when finished, I, too, look like road kill.

I lay them in the sun to dry,
Then store them in a cool place,
Out of sight of the anxious eyes and eager reach
Of all the hungry squirrels
Secretly watching and thanking me.
Now, you might think, it's time to get cracking.
But wait! We must give the nuts
Time to age and mature.

This will only take a year.

Let's be clear. The Black Walnut is not our friend.
It is not like the prissy English Walnut:
Lovely, refined, and easy to crack,
With lovely nut meat that just falls out
Intact in your hand
With a sweet, smooth, sublime flavor.
No, the Black Walnut is one stubborn American,
The English Walnut's rebellious cousin,
Hard to crack and with a wild, unique taste,
Like local moonshine, venison, and liver mush.
It's a flavor as strong as its shell and
With a taste that must be acquired.
Few do. I regret I have.

When I'm in the rare mood to crack Black Walnuts
I first gather my instruments
Like an old "sawbones" surgeon
Who prepares to amputate a wounded soldier's leg
By hacking through his femur:
Sledgehammer, small pointed spear/pick,
(I'm sure it has a more appropriate name)
My two-pronged squeezer/cracker
    …aka finger smasher,
And of course, a very small bowl,
For there won't be much nut meat for it to hold.

There is no best way to best crack a Black Walnut.
Its shell is harder than fossilized
Ivory Bill woodpecker lips,

And more frustrating to crack than a Rubic's Cube.
It is a fact that it is best to go at them
When you have need to bust someone's head open.
I go at them on a tall, hard stump
And with an attitude.
Right after a fight with my wife
Is the best time to start.
It's the same stump my old uncle used to
Cut off the chicken's head for Sunday dinner.
It's the execution stump.

I don't go at it gently, carefully.
It won't let me, won't cooperate,
Won't respect me.
I have to be mean, assertive, aggressive.
It might respect me a little then,
But it still won't help me out.
My angle of attack makes no difference.
A whack at either end or sideways
Will produce the same outcome,
Nothing much.

The stump is close to the fire pit, too.
I throw the empty shells there.
It feels good casting them
Into the pit of hell fire and brimstone,
Their just reward for making me work so damn hard.

Thankfully, the cracking process does require me
To cuss, swear, sip whiskey, smoke cigars,
Chase errant pieces,
Probe shells with a spear,
Eat a great many small pieces
I should keep for later, and even bust a finger or two.
Finally, I've cracked all the nuts
I so diligently collected and worked thru the year.
Now, I'll just relax, sit in front of the fireplace, and
Sip a little steel-horse whiskey while savoring that unique taste
Of my home-grown Black Walnuts.

But from where I sit and write this,
I see that old Black Walnut
In the saddle of those pasture slopes,
Reminding me that a new fall is here.
It points to the ground around it
Where a new batch of Black Walnuts lie,
Insists I come pick them up, and start again.
But, I keep thinking about that pond.

After the Hunt

I sit alone by the stone fire pit
As evening shadows ease away to the east.
Tired dogs rest in the grass, chew sticks,
And click-mouth hard hickory nuts.
On time, a slight wind rises from the bottom.
The dogs nose it and with eyes closed,
Sort creek water from deer.
The wood bench and broken chairs are vacant,
Stump seats are back at the woodpile.
They all keep me company and share the silence
Which holds secret
The wild lies, belches, and flatulence
That caused harmless curses, swearing, and laughs.
Tamped down grass won't recover soon.
There is a faint smell of whiskey,
Stale beer, and dead fire.
A careless bottle, kicked over and forgotten,
Hides under a broken chair,
Both well used and abused.
Stuck between stones, a wet-chewed cigar
Sticks up like a middle finger.
I see them all sitting there in the dark,
Firelight painting their faces a ghostly youth.
Leaves scratch down the slope of the tin roof
And familiar stars quietly join in.
The dogs grow restless and soon
We'll walk the slow walk to the house.

Partisan Patrol

We crossed the tracks in single file,
Mindful of imagined enemy trains from either end:
Quiet, determined, partisans on patrol.
The small pine grove rose like an island
On the field's horizon,
Shouldered the long, straight track
Which cut through like a zipper.

We made our way there and inside
Found a worn trail with soft pine straw beds,
Tempting a much-needed rest.
The path rose gently toward
An opening to the field.
There, the one in front froze.
His arm held me back.

Ahead, a large snake lay coiled in the path,
Content in a patch of autumn sun.
A careful look told us it was not a threat.
It had no poison and sadly, would not run.
It rose cobra-like, spread its throat,
Defiant and threatening. But,
We could easily move around,

Leave him in the warm sun to enjoy his meal of
Field mice which lumped in his length.
This I much preferred and encouraged.
But my fellow partisans had not my heart

And the poor creature succumbed to their assault,
His strength and nobility stolen,
His head slowly settled in death.

They proceeded on, left it with their indifference.
I lagged and secretly gathered him up,
Took him along and later, jarred him in alcohol.
It had found that island of pines a refuge,
As did I. But we could not share it.
I learned early that you cannot
Share things with a snake.

Under the Osage

We buried her on the hill under the Osage.
It is where she asked to be.
She liked the old tree,
Only one in the county she'd say.

And the forester confirmed this each fall
When he came to collect seeds,
Which he tried to grow, but never could.
With each of his visits
We learned more about the Osage:

How tough its wood, best for slinging arrows,
Making good hedges, and fence posts which last.
And the unique color of its wood is
Highly desired for its many uses,
Beauty, and strength.

But Yellow Jackets nested at the head of her grave,
And through summer, kept our flowers away.

An attempt at a Elizabethan sonnet and a little truth.

Thank you for reading
Under the Helix Kelpies

Please post a review on Amazon.com
and
check out other books by Michael R. Howard

The Lightning and the Gale
And
The Impeded Stream

Acknowledgments

This book was not possible without the generous help and support of all my fellow poets in our Laura (Riding) Jackson Foundation's *Porch Poets* and *Poets Corner* writing groups. As always, my Editor, Susan Lovelace, and Publisher, Janet Sierzant, deserve my high praise and eternal thanks for making my work and this book better. And special thanks to Indian River County Poet Laureate Patricia Draper for her willingness to suffer through my work and write such kind words about it.

The poems "Brown Dogs in a Green Field" and "Under the Helix Kelpies" were finalists in the 2024 Florida Writers Association's annual Royal Palm Literary Awards.

The poem "Feral Kid" was a Semi-Finalist in the 2024 Florida Writers Association's annual Royal Palm Literary Awards.

www.ingramcontent.com/pod-product-compliance
Lightning Source LLC
Chambersburg PA
CBHW030004050426
42451CB00006B/112